Mike,

May God inspire your life as He has inspired mine.

Joe

5 a.m. with Jesus

JOSEPH R. HORNSBY

WESTBOW
PRESS®
A DIVISION OF THOMAS NELSON
& ZONDERVAN

Copyright © 2016 Joseph R. Hornsby.

All rights reserved. No part of this book may be used or reproduced by any means, graphic, electronic, or mechanical, including photocopying, recording, taping or by any information storage retrieval system without the written permission of the author except in the case of brief quotations embodied in critical articles and reviews.

This book is a work of non-fiction. Unless otherwise noted, the author and the publisher make no explicit guarantees as to the accuracy of the information contained in this book and in some cases, names of people and places have been altered to protect their privacy.

Scripture taken from the Holy Bible, NEW INTERNATIONAL VERSION®. Copyright © 1973, 1978, 1984 by Biblica, Inc. All rights reserved worldwide. Used by permission. NEW INTERNATIONAL VERSION® and NIV® are registered trademarks of Biblica, Inc. Use of either trademark for the offering of goods or services requires the prior written consent of Biblica US, Inc.

WestBow Press books may be ordered through booksellers or by contacting:

WestBow Press
A Division of Thomas Nelson & Zondervan
1663 Liberty Drive
Bloomington, IN 47403
www.westbowpress.com
1 (866) 928-1240

Because of the dynamic nature of the Internet, any web addresses or links contained in this book may have changed since publication and may no longer be valid. The views expressed in this work are solely those of the author and do not necessarily reflect the views of the publisher, and the publisher hereby disclaims any responsibility for them.

Any people depicted in stock imagery provided by Thinkstock are models, and such images are being used for illustrative purposes only.
Certain stock imagery © Thinkstock.

ISBN: 978-1-5127-3534-5 (sc)
ISBN: 978-1-5127-3535-2 (hc)
ISBN: 978-1-5127-3533-8 (e)

Library of Congress Control Number: 2016904606

Print information available on the last page.

WestBow Press rev. date: 04/27/2016

Psalm 5:3

In the morning, Lord, you hear my voice; in the morning I lay my requests before you and wait expectantly.

5 a.m. with Jesus

5 a.m. with Jesus
Is the perfect time, to me
For seeking out His presence
It's the best place I can be
I love reading from His Word
He has many things to say
Jesus makes me feel special
By blessing me, each day
5 a.m. with Jesus
Before the break of day
Before the world awakens
It is peaceful, as I pray
I tell Jesus, all my worries
The desires of my heart
We watch as the sun rises
As another new day starts
5 a.m. with Jesus
The Holy Spirit inspires me
I write down these thoughts
For other people to see
The words are not my own
I'll give credit, where credit's due
The words are from a higher source
Through my heart, just for you

Psalm 39:1

I said, "I will watch my ways and keep my tongue from sin; I will put a muzzle on my mouth while in the presence of the wicked."

Your Tongue

Your tongue is your rudder
Your direction is what you utter
Your tongue can steer you right
Or it can steer you wrong
It can provoke a fight
With words, sharp and strong
It can turn love into hate
Or turn one's faith into doubt
Your tongue can cause your fate
From the statements that come out
Speak of goodness, hope, and blessings
When life deals out hard lessons
Speak positive and you will see
Your life will have more harmony

Matthew 24:36

But about that day or hour no one knows, not even the angels in heaven, nor the Son, but only the Father.

The Old Sign in The Tree

I take the same road to work, everyday
See the same scenery along the way
Dodge the same potholes, make the same stops
Speeding right along, watching out for cops
I see an old sign in a tree as I drive by
I read its words every morning, no lie
It took a misfortune, an inconvenient day
Before I understood what those words really say
For years, I've been down on my luck
I was fed up with life, my wife, and old truck
Then one day my truck broke, at a bad time
Feeling sorry, I looked up, and saw that sign
Of all the places, how could this be
There was that old sign in the tree
As I read it's words, I looked at the sky
Then tears began to fall from my eyes
I thought, how I've lived life all wrong
How empty I've felt for too long
So, beneath that old sign in the tree
I prayed to the Lord to come rescue me
About the time, right out of the blue
A man drove up and knew what to do
Soon, my truck ran, after connecting a wire
I was amazed, how the whole thing transpired
I stared at that old sign, hard and long

The answer had been there, all along
The real truth and I read the sign again
Then I asked God to forgive my sins
I've never been the same, now, I pray
And I still see that old sign, everyday
Three words, so powerful and true
I pray they will change your whole life, too
"Jesus Is Coming," said the old sign in the tree
I tell you, Jesus sure did come for me
He is real, He lives deep in my heart
So, if you're fed up and need a new start
Call out to Jesus, He will come to you
Jesus is coming. Yes, He's coming for you

Psalm 32:7

You are my hiding place; you will protect me from trouble and surround me with songs of deliverance.

Shade of My Love

Made in the image of Me
An apple doesn't fall far from the tree
I knew you, before your birth
You blossomed, became fruit, then fell to earth
The world picked you up, took you from Me
You changed from who I made you to be
Now, you're lonely, empty, and abused
The world beat you up, now, you're bruised
Come back to Me, I'll make you like new
You'll become fruitful, I will restore you
I'm still here, watching you from above
Come live in the shade of my love

Romans 1:17

For in the gospel the righteousness of God is revealed-a righteousness that is by faith from first to last, just as it is written: "The righteous will live by faith."

Granny's Bible

We went back to her house
After her funeral had ended
It became a family reunion
All my relatives attended
We were eating and talking
Catching up on our lives
In the living room were the men
In the kitchen were the wives
I quietly went upstairs
To her bedroom to reminisce
About my past as a child
Gone are those days that I truly miss
I sat on her old bed
Looked in the nightstand drawer
There was her Holy Bible
She read to me many times before
I picked up her worn out book
Thumbed through the tattered pages
Many scriptures were underlined
She had marked through the ages
I was shocked, when I discovered
A bookmarker I had made when I was five
I started to weep
Wishing she were alive

When I grew up I moved far away
To make it in this world on my own
The times we shared had ended
I'm sad knowing she lived alone
But now she lives in Heaven above
A place where I plan to see
I'll do my best to live by her example
So Granny will be proud of me
She left behind her greatest treasure
More valuable than any gold I'd say
I will cherish, my Granny's old Bible
And live by its words, everyday

Psalm 51:17

My sacrifice, O God, is a broken spirit; a broken and contrite heart you, God, will not despise.

Broken

Broken
I came here broken
My heart is in pieces
I have nowhere to turn
I am ashamed, unworthy
With all that remains
Take what is left, Lord
Every broken piece
Only you can help me
Make everything new
I have little to offer
But what I have is Yours
My faith is in You
As I leave from here
This place of surrender
I'm expecting a miracle
That is my hope
As I rise and walk away
I leave behind on the altar
All of my chains
Broken

Psalm 119:59

I have considered my ways and have turned my steps to your statutes.

Every Reason

I once had every reason
To keep You far from Me
I stayed away, best I could
Believing I was free
I lived as I pleased
But suffered for my ways
Although You still loved me
My heart pushed You away
God, You had every reason
To stop loving me
Yet You never gave up
This truth I can see
My closed heart opened up
I cried, "God, come on in"
You entered and changed me
Forgave me of every sin
Now, I have every reason
To love You everyday
I seek You every morning
You listen, while I pray
The lost child, the loving Father
A happy ending to my story
Yes, God is every reason
To live for Him and for His glory

Romans 8:28

And we know that in all things God works for the good of those who love him, who have been called according to his purpose.

Everything Will Be All Right

When bad storms form, I believe
Everything will be all right
When chaos comes, I believe
Everything will be all right
My Lord is near, a prayer away
He comforts me, He saves the day
Jesus loves me, I always say
Everything will be all right
When I am sick, I believe
Everything will be all right
When plans don't work, I believe
Everything will be all right
My Lord is near, a prayer away
He comforts me, He saves the day
Jesus loves me, I always say
Everything will be all right
When trouble knocks, I believe
Everything will be all right
When I fail in life, I believe
Everything will be all right
My Lord is near, a prayer away
He comforts me, He saves the day
Jesus loves me, I always say
Everything will be all right

Proverbs 4:1

Listen, my sons, to a father's instruction; pay attention and gain understanding.

What Every Son Longs to Hear

He looks at his father laying quietly in bed
Wondering, if he hears anything that's said
"Dad, can you hear me? It's good to see you."
"Dad, is there something I can do for you?"

But his father only stares, as if no one's around
No facial movement, just a frozen frown
Is this how it ends after a long fruitful life
After working and providing for his family and wife

He flips through the memories, written on his mind
To the days with his father, back in younger times
He wishes he was successful, had made his father proud
Instead of living as a fool, doing things not allowed

He has changed, since then, his head is on straight
He has Jesus in his heart and that changed his fate
He can't erase the past, nor the heartaches made
Not once did his father's love ever fade

He leans over the bed to give his father a goodbye kiss
The hugs he once felt, now he will miss
He says, "Dad, I'll be back. Dad, I love you."
Then he hears in a whisper, "Son, I'm proud of you."

Psalm 119:105

Your word is a lamp for my feet, a light on my path.

Footsteps, In Faith

I take my footsteps, in faith
Trusting God's Word and grace
Believing He will lead me through
Every tribulation I'll face

I'll stumble along the way
But I know I will prevail
Because Jesus goes before
I'm certain, I will not fail

With Christ, there're no options
Victory's waiting at the end
When my footsteps stop here
Heaven's where they'll begin

I pray to God as I travel
Down in valleys and up the slopes
I walk with footsteps in faith
For faith is the eyes of my hope

Luke 6:31

Do unto others as you would have them do to you.

Love One Another

Here we are
So close, yet too far
Like a twinkling star
That we wish upon
What will it take
Still, we make mistakes
Stop, for our own sake
For peace and love to dawn

Love one another, has been said
Written scriptures have been read
Still, there is hate
Love one another, let's join hands
Let compassion grow and span
And change our fate

There's no gain
Causing others pain
War and blood does stain
And it's hard to erase
Time to start
Let's light up the dark
With love, from our hearts
A thought to embrace

Deuteronomy 4:29

You will find him if you seek him with all your heart and with all your soul.

My Time with Jesus

I went to see Jesus outside the city
I was amazed at the large crowd
People were yelling and shoving each other
The noise grew extremely loud
From their responses, I knew He was teaching
I couldn't hear Him from where I stood
Then people shouted, "Hosanna! Hosanna!"
His message must have been good
I thought, "I wish I was closer
So, I could hear what He had to say."
Like a miracle, the sea of people parted
Which made a straight pathway
His stare at me was piercing
I felt something come over me
I heard in my mind, Him calling
I went to Him and fell to my knees
With tears on my face, I felt unworthy
I would have run away, if only I could
He came closer and whispered in my ear
His words to my heart felt good
He said,
"I am the Way, the Life, and the Truth
Let this moment be a sign of proof
From this day, trust Me, in all you do
Follow Me and believe, I love you."

1 Chronicles 16:11

Look to the Lord and his strength; seek his face always.

I Need You, Jesus

I need You, Jesus
Please, comfort me
My heart is broken
From this tragedy
I can't stop crying
Can't understand
This is life changing
But not as I planned
I need You, Jesus
Joy has left me
Why did this happen
How can this be
The enemy broke through
My line of defense
I'm at a loss, Lord
This doesn't make sense
I need You, Jesus
Now, as I grieve
My hope's with You
In this, I believe
I'm filled with sorrow
When will this end
I need You, Jesus
To know joy again

Psalm 9:10

Those who know your name trust in you, for you, Lord, have never forsaken those who seek you.

Why I Climb

I'm climbing up
Another rugged mountain
I'm on my way
To see Jesus, my Lord
The path is steep
But not so steep to stop me
I'll keep climbing
To see Jesus, my Lord
I'm looking up, as I climb
I'm praising Him, as I climb
Jesus loves me
That's why I climb
He is my Light, as I climb
My soul shines, as I climb
Jesus loves me
That's why I climb
Then, when I reach
This rugged mountain's peak
I will give thanks
To Jesus Christ, my Lord
And if there stands
Another mountain in the way
I'll keep on climbing
To see Jesus, my Lord

Psalm 119:81

My soul faints with longing for your salvation, but I have put my hope in your word.

Words for My Soul

My God loves me
He's written me instructions
Words for my soul
To keep me safe and sound
Before the sun
Rises, each morning
I read His words
They help me stand my ground
His words are hope
I hide them in my heart
They bless my soul
Words for my soul
They give me light
When blinded by the dark
They bless my soul
Words for my soul
Thank You, my God
For writing these love letters
They comfort me
During times of fear
I'll treasure them
Always, forever
Words for my soul
Truthful and sincere

Isaiah 40:31

But those who hope in the Lord will renew their strength. They will soar on wings like eagles; they will run and not grow weary, they will walk and not be faint.

I'll Never Fly Solo

I have dreams on my mind
And desires in my heart
I'm heading skyward
I'm ready to start
Life tries to hold me down
But faith will lift me high
I'll ask Jesus for help
As I learn how to fly
I'll never fly solo
Jesus flies with me
He is my pilot
Heaven is my destiny
With Him in my life
I can do all things
I can't wait to fly
And see what the future brings
There's a message I'll share
Good News from above
Of a Savior I know
With the only perfect love
His Word is my wind
When I take off and fly
I will not live in fear
When I soar the sky

Isaiah 58:8

Then your light will break forth like dawn, and your healing will quickly appear; then your righteousness will go before you, and the glory of the Lord will be your rear guard.

Healing Prayer

My Lord,
You know my heart
The pain and sorrow I feel
You see my tears that fall
Hear my pleas, please heal

Place Your hand on my life
Strengthen me, I am weak
Help me see the way to go
Send me the hope I seek

I put all my trust in You, Lord
For You are faithful to me
Your love has no limits
It comforts my misery

I look for joy in the morning
And mercy with the rising sun
But tonight, I need your peace
Knowing soon my healing will come

1 Corinthians 15:57

But thanks be to God! He gives us the victory through our Lord Jesus Christ.

I Walk In Victory

Though there's dirt in my eyes
And I can't see things clear
I walk in victory
And give thanks Jesus is near

Though I've scars on my life
From battles in the past
I walk in victory
For I found Jesus at last

Though I stumble and fall
I step right back in place
I walk in victory
For I trust God gives grace

Though I'm weak in my will
There is mercy from above
I walk in victory
Because of Jesus and His love

Psalm 58:7

Let them vanish like water that flows away; when they draw the bow, let their arrows fall short.

I Will Not Yield

He is my hope, my inspiration
I turn to Him, he protects me
I will not quit, never surrender
I'll stand and fight for my victory
Christ is my strength
He is my shield
I will not yield
No, I will not yield
My foes will fail
I will prevail
I will not yield
No, I will not yield
When arrows fly to pierce my soul
They will fall short of their mark
I'm not alone, He's fighting with me
He made a promise, I keep in my heart
Christ is my strength
He is my shield
I will not yield
No, I will not yield
My foes will fail
I will prevail
I will not yield
No, I will not yield

Isaiah 45:3

I will give you hidden treasures, riches stored in secret places, so that you may know that I am the Lord, the God of Israel, who summons you by name.

He Shares His Wealth with My Soul

Each morning I seek the Lord before I start
We talk of things that weigh on my heart
He listens and strengthens my faith to see
All worry leaves and peace comes to me

I treasure my time with the Lord
His presence gives me great reward
His love is better than any gold
He shares His wealth with my soul
A rich man, I'll always remain
Since I've known Him, I'm not the same
Jesus made my poor life whole
He shares His wealth with my soul

I love Him, I know, He loves me more
He encourages me, I'm better than before
Each evening I thank Him, then I sleep
I trust Him, my soul is His to keep

Proverbs 3:1

My son, do not forget my teachings, but keep my commands in your heart,

I Will Do My Best

I'm going to keep on trying
Until I get it right
If today I should fail
Lord, forgive me tonight
I'll ask for God's help
Every morning as I pray
I will do my best
To live the Lord's way
There are mountains to climb
And valleys to cross
I'll move forward each day
Try again, when there's loss
God's Word is my guide
His precepts I'll obey
I will do my best
To walk the Lord's way
When my journey's over
And my body is frail
I know Heaven is ahead
At the end of the trail
When I go before God
I hope to hear Him say
Well done, faithful servant
Welcome home, walk this way

Matthew 18:20

For where two or three gather in my name, there am I with them.

A Prayer for You

When I woke this morning
My first thought was of you
Your bad news really struck me
When you hurt, I hurt too
You're not alone, as you worry
If you're scared, I understand
Together, we'll fight your problem
Are you ready, then take my hand

I'm going to say a prayer for you
I believe in my heart it will go through
Have trust and faith you're going to win
Let's keep praying until then
Don't let this problem get you down
A prayer for you is heaven bound
Victory is yours to claim, my friend
Let's keep praying until then

I know the Lord will be with you
When two or more pray together
In Your name, Jesus, we ask You
Please, help my friend get better
I won't pray for you, just one time
I'll continue tomorrow, too
I can't get you off my mind
Nor my heart, cause I love you

Proverbs 15:31

Whoever heeds life-giving correction will be at home among the wise.

A Happy Ending

I was given four pages of life
Not many, though it could be less
Four pages, to do what I wished
My destiny would be anybody's guess

The first page was my childhood
Full of fantasies and vivid dreams
I was naïve and became disillusioned
Reality happened different, from my dreams

Those youthful days were exciting
Happiness was a place in the sun
Worries were short, soon forgotten
Every day was meant to have fun

As I turned to the second page
I thought I knew it all
But failure came and I stumbled
Frustrated and disgusted with each fall

Growing older, I became more confused
I couldn't think, how to make my life work
I was angry and bitter, completely lost
Then my anger with time, turned into hurt

After reaching the first line on page three
I realized the errors of my ways
I tried undoing what I had done
To make up for all those lost days

Instead of chasing things of this world
I separated myself from their pull
I humbled my life before God
Started changing, from being a fool

Page four is quickly approaching
With little time left for spending
I'm using God's words of wisdom
So, my story has a happy ending

Proverbs 22:6

Start children off on the way they should go, and even when they are old they will not turn from it.

God and Granny

Back in the days of my youth
Granny taught me about God's truth
From her old Bible she would read
Teaching me lessons I would need

I didn't know until I was grown
All the good seeds she had sown
Now, I produce good fruit from them
God blesses me and I'm blessing Him

God and Granny knew how life would be
Their wisdom has put wisdom in me
I understand every scripture I heard
Her voice still echoes God's Word

Granny's gone to her heavenly home
I'm doing well, but I'm not alone
I have three children and a lovely wife
I'm truly blessed, Yes, I'm rich in my life

I train my children, as I was raised
To love God and give Him praise
I read to them the Bible stories, I was read
And say our prayers, then go to bed

Psalm 34:18

The lord is close to the brokenhearted and saves those who are crushed in spirit.

Broken Shells

He combs the beach at morning
Searching for broken shells
Large or small, He loves them all
He puts them in His pail
Not a single shell is perfect
Each one has a flaw
But He knows them and their beauty
That no one before ever saw
Wonderful and amazing
Is His collection, kept back home
All these old broken shells
He now calls His own
When my life here is over
And my purpose is no more
I believe God will take me home
His broken shell, from the shore

Psalm 4:1

Answer me when I call to you, my righteous God. Give me relief from my distress; have mercy on me and hear my prayer.

Hear My Prayer

Hear my prayer, Lord
I trust You are there
Hear my prayer, Lord
I am in Your care
Have mercy for me
Please, turn my way
I need You, Lord
Listen, as I pray
You know my sickness
You know my fears
You know my troubles
You've seen my tears
You know my shame
Lord, set me free
I'm calling You
Jesus, save me
Hear my prayer, Lord
I am in despair
Hear my prayer, Lord
Life's been unfair
You are my hope
Show me the way
I need You, Lord
Listen, as I pray

Psalm 119:11

I have hidden your word in my heart that I might not sin against you.

Your Word

The reading of Your Word gives light
I seek it each day for sight
It brings joy and peace to my soul
It's truth and wisdom makes me whole
Your Word makes me fruitful in my deeds
It yields a great harvest from its seeds
I planted it in the soil of my heart
Where it took root, right from the start
Your Word leads me to Eternity
With faith in Your Word, I can see

1 John 3:1

See what great love the Father has lavished on us, that we should be called children of god! And that is what we are! The reason the world does not know us is that it did not know him.

Beautiful, Perfect Love

Jesus, I want to tell You
I've never done this before
I find as my life passes
I need You, more and more
I want a relationship
To grow closer to You, each day
My heart has a new passion
Come into my life and stay
Now that I have found You
I never want to leave
Your love means everything
That's what I believe
There are no greater gifts
That I'll ever know of
I am grateful I know You
And Your beautiful, perfect love

Matthew 5:10

Blessed are those who are persecuted because of righteousness, for theirs is the kingdom of heaven.

Glory to Jesus

They can't kill Jesus
Why do they still try
Their efforts are useless
Our Savior can't die
Why do they hate Him
His message of love
Love is the answer
We need more of
Glory to Jesus
Give glory to Christ
He proved, He loved us
Through His sacrifice
Glory to Jesus
All glory to Him
His glory shines bright
It never will dim
They may kill Christians
We'll die in His Name
Jesus is King
We proudly proclaim
Fools fight against us
Our blood's on their swords
Still, victory is ours
Through Jesus, our Lord

Hebrews 11:6

And without faith it is impossible to please God, because anyone who comes to him must believe that he exists and that he rewards those who earnestly seek him.

Faith Conquers Fear

What are you going to do
Your debts, you cannot pay
But you've got to eat, so eat
Then pray, you've got to pray
Lean hard on your faith
For it draws God near
Trust Him, with all of your heart
Believe, faith conquers fear
What are you going to do
A loved one lies in a death bed
You've heard, nothing can be done
Sad thoughts, fill your head
Cling fast to your faith
For it draws God near
Trust Him, with all of your heart
Believe, faith conquers fear
What are you going to do
Love in your marriage changed
The one you're married to
Has started acting strange
Lift up high your faith
For it draws God near
Trust Him, with all your heart
Believe, faith conquers fear

Hebrews 6:19

We have this hope as an anchor for the soul, firm and secure. It enters the inner sanctuary behind the curtain,

The Anchor of My Soul

The water pounds against my bow
As my weak vessel struggles each day
In my journey, bad storms have passed
But I don't fear, instead I pray

I still have hope, when skies look dreary
I ask for guidance, when I lose control
I find new strength, when I grow weary
All from the Anchor of my soul

I've nearly crashed upon the rocks
Almost drowned in the rough sea
I could have died, but I'm alive
I found Jesus and He saved me

Jesus is my hope, when skies look dreary
Jesus helps me, when I lose control
Jesus is strength, when I grow weary
Jesus is the Anchor of my soul

Romans 1:17

For in the gospel the righteousness of God is revealed, a righteousness that is by faith from first to last, just as it is written: "The righteous will live by faith."

Live by Faith

Live by faith
Not by sight
Hope is found
In God's light
Live for today
Let go of tomorrow
Use what you have
Don't try to borrow
Give of yourself
To unfortunate others
Obey God
Also, your mother
Life is short
Here on earth
Be a servant
Be of worth
Trust in God
And Jesus, His Son
Live by faith
For blessings to come

1 Peter 1:3

Praise be to the God and Father of our Lord Jesus Christ! In his great mercy he has given us new birth into a living hope through the resurrection of Jesus Christ from the dead,

I See New Mercy

I see new mercy
Coming with dawn
Time for rejoicing
Soon, darkness is gone
Hope is arriving
I welcome this day
God, my Provider
He makes a way
I have new mercy
More of God's grace
He will be with me
As I run my race
If I should stumble
Fall down and fail
He will forgive me
Love always prevails
I need new mercy
To start off each day
Unworthy, but grateful
I thank God and pray

1 Timothy 6:17

Command those who are rich in this present world not to be arrogant nor to put their hope in wealth, which is so uncertain, but to put their hope in God, who richly provides us with everything for our enjoyment.

God Is My Gold

God is my gold
A treasure of pure love
Nothing has greater value
That I can think of

How much richer am I
Having all my faith in Him
What more do I need
My cup overflows its brim

I will die a wealthy man
With an inheritance to leave
To my children, this gift of gold
My God, whom I believe

Psalm 84:3

Even the sparrow has found a home, and the swallow a nest for herself, where she may have her young- a place near your altar, Lord Almighty, my King and my God.

Like A Sparrow

Like a sparrow lives each day
Whom seems happy, I would say
Singing praises at sunrise
Before taking to the skies

Like a sparrow building a nest
To have a family and be blessed
Surviving storms, as it lives
Singing daily, for all God gives

Like a sparrow I want to be
Filled with joy, living free
Trusting God for everything
Whose grateful heart always sings

Like a sparrow I will sing
No matter what tomorrow brings
For God is good, He's in control
Into His hands I place my soul

2 Timothy 3:12

In fact, everyone who wants to live a godly life in Christ Jesus will be persecuted,

I Am a Christian

I am a Christian
My life will proclaim
I'm willing to die
To advance His Name
Though the enemy comes
To destroy, steal, and kill
Still, I'll have victory
Doing God's will
I am a Christian
I must confess
I live, serving Him
Dying, as nothing less
I hope with strong faith
Of seeing tomorrow
Either, here or in Heaven
If Heaven, free of sorrow
I am a Christian
I carry my cross
I'll follow Jesus
No matter, the cost
I praise Him, at dawn
I thank Him, at night
If I die, today
Forever, I'll see His Light

1 Peter 1:21

Through him you believe in God, who raised him from the dead and glorified him, and so your faith and hope are in God.

Believe, Have Faith, and Pray

You're not alone, He is with you
You may not see Him, but He's there
Like the sun rising at daybreak
You'll see Him move, if you stare
He'll talk to you in a small voice
That speaks volumes in your life
But you'll have to stop and listen
Concentrate on Him, not strife
The things you don't see can save you
Like someone you didn't know
Who loved you first and died for you
On a cross, long time ago
The life you've lived has hurt you
You're looking for a happy day
You don't see Him, but you'll feel Him
So, believe, have faith, and pray
The whole world has gone crazy
Chaos's thriving everywhere
Don't get caught up in the storm
There's still hope and peace out there
Call to Him, He's your answer
The calm in this hurricane
As the walls around you crumble
Stand in victory, praise His Name

Micah 7:7

But as for me, I watch in hope for the lord, I wait for God my Savior; my God will hear me.

Pray and Be Still

I know your pain
Been where you are
I've felt the same
I bear the scar
It hurts inside
I know, my friend
If you'll hang on
This trial will end
My word for you
So, you will heal
Turn to the Lord
Pray and be still
I see your tears
Have left their mark
Your face reveals
Your broken heart
I will help you
To find your way
Let's close our eyes
My friend, and pray

Luke 15:4

"Suppose one of you has a hundred sheep and loses one of them. Doesn't he leave the ninety-nine in the open country and go after the lost sheep until he finds it?"

I Am Grateful, I Know Jesus

I am grateful, I know Jesus
I am glad that He found me
I was lost among the hopeless
All the ones, too blind to see

I know He heard me in the darkness
Crying, wishing I could die
He must have felt my heart aching
Breaking, every time I tried

I am grateful, I know Jesus
He saved me from myself
When I thought I was a lost cause
He knew I was someone else

I gave to Him my aching heart
Along with my life and soul
He took all of my broken pieces
Somehow, Jesus made me whole

Psalm 66:16

Come and hear, all you who fear God; let me tell you what he has done for me.

Your Way

I thank You, my Lord
For another day
Before I go out
Listen, as I pray
You're good to me
Yes, I'm truly blessed
I would still praise You
Lord, if I had much less
When I look back
From where I came from
The miracles I've had
Seeing all You have done
If I died today
I trust where I will go
But there are those, Lord
Unsure, who don't know
Lord, let there be one
One lost soul this day
That's touched by my soul
And wants to know Your way

Isaiah 41:6

They help each other and say to their companions, "Be strong!"

Don't Give Up, Friend

Don't you give up
Hold on, an answer's coming
Better days are waiting up ahead
I'll pray for you
Soon you'll have your breakthrough
Trust in God and every word, He said

You've come this far
You'll make it all the way
Don't give up, friend
Don't give up, friend
I'm here for you
I'm here with you, to pray
Don't give up, friend
Don't give up, friend

If not today
Have hope for tomorrow
You're closer to the answer you desire
Believe in God
Faith is the substance hoped for
Tomorrow, your breakthrough will transpire

Psalm 39:7

But now, Lord, what do I look for? My hope is in you.

When Tears Ain't Enough

When tears ain't enough
To get rid of my pain
After I cry me a river
I call out His Name
Jesus is my hope
He is my sunshine
To push through the clouds
And ease my troubled mind
When tears ain't enough
To remove my despair
I pray to Jesus
I send Him a prayer
Jesus is my hope
He is my sunshine
To push through the clouds
And ease my troubled mind
When tears ain't enough
After crying all night
I ask for new mercy
To come with dawn's light
Jesus is my hope
He is my sunshine
To push through the clouds
And ease my troubled mind
Shine, Jesus shine, dry up my tears
Put joy in my heart, end all my fears

Numbers 12:6

He said, "Listen to my words: "when there is a prophet among you, I, the Lord, reveal myself to them in visions, I speak to them in dreams.

A Dream for Tomorrow

God gave certain men
A dream for all mankind
To carry out God's plan
For precious is the time
But mankind listens to
Another tempting voice
Hate continues to thrive
And dreams die by choice
Why is there still hate
Why do we have to kill
How can peace ever live
When blood is what we spill
Peace could come to life
And be not just a dream
God's Word tells us how
For peace to be redeemed
Father, please give again
A dream for tomorrow
Father, please forgive us
Save us, from our sorrow

Romans 5:8

But God demonstrates his own love for us in this: While we were still sinners, Christ died for us.

Jesus, Make Me Whole

It is hard
Harder, than I thought
To believe
That's not how I was taught
Daddy told me
Which I think he told me wrong
There's no God
Believe in yourself to be strong
I'm at a place
A broken shell of a man
Crying like a baby
Cause life didn't go as planned
So, if You're up there
Looking down on me
Help me, Lord, please
My soul's in misery
I don't deserve it
Looking at me at first glance
But I am sorry
Lord, I need another chance
If You'll forgive me
And come into my heart
I'd be grateful to You
Today, I'm ready to start

There's been something
Missing in my life
It wasn't love
That came from my wife
It goes much deeper
Deep as my aching soul
I need You, I know
Jesus, make me whole

1 Timothy 5:5

The widow who is really in need and left all alone puts her hope in God and continues night and day to pray and ask God for help.

Have Hope and Pray

Friend, I can tell
Your eyes can't hide your pain
Like clouds, they are
Ready to pour down rain
Rain, if you must
Not every day is blue skies
Healing begins
After your soul cries

Have hope and pray
Miracles are on their way
Have hope and pray
Yes, they're on their way

Friend, I believe
Your life will be made right
Trust in God's help
Let faith, become your sight
Sure as the sun
Will shine on us tomorrow
You'll smile again
Gone will be your sorrow

Matthew 15:25

The woman came and knelt before him. "Lord, help me!" she said.

We Better Get Jesus, Now

Someone has gotten themselves
In deep trouble, once again
They've tried to find a way
To escape the pit they're in
Or a doctor comes in some room
With results that show bad news
He says there's choices to make
But there's only one to choose
We better get Jesus, now
This ain't going to fix itself
He's our only hope for this
We've tried everything else
There's a higher power to use
When the future's looking grim
We better get Jesus, now
Everybody, let's pray for Him
The world is in a terrible mess
Chaos is everywhere you look
Seems like, we're heading for hell
Cause we ain't living by the Book
Right is wrong and wrong is right
Our forecast is looking dark
We better let in the Light
Let Jesus dwell in our hearts

We better get Jesus, now
This ain't going to fix itself
He's our only hope for this
We've tried, everything else
There's a higher power to use
When the future is looking grim
We better get Jesus, now
Everybody, let's pray for Him

Psalm 107:14

He brought them out of darkness, the utter darkness, and broke away their chains.

The Love You Have for Me

Lead me, Jesus
Out of the dark
Let me see hope, once again
My heart's heavy
From tribulations
Will these trials ever end

I've talked to others
Who say, they know You
Their hearts seem happy
With joy, I wish I knew
I've lived without knowing
But it's time to see
The joy of loving You
And the love You have for me

Help me, Jesus
Out of the dark
I keep falling down in shame
I'm unworthy
To ask You for help
But Jesus, I'm calling Your Name

Hebrews 11:1

Now faith is confidence in what we hope for and assurance about what we do not see.

You're Going to Fly

You've made a list
Before you die
You're going to leap
You're going to fly
But you can't live
Safe on ground
Clinging to fear
That you'll fall down
Where is your faith
You keep talking of
To leap off cliffs
And fly above
Go, spread your wings
And say a prayer
Leap toward God
He'll take it from there

1 John 4:4

You, dear children, are from God and have overcome them, because the one who is in you is greater than the one who is in the world.

Ain't No One Like Jesus

Who would go through
Hell, just to save me
Torture, to save you
Jesus did
Who would forgive
Sinners of all kinds
Have mercy for their lives
Jesus did
Ain't no one like Jesus
Nor will there be one
He is our Savior
He is God's Son
No one will ever
Love us like He can
He's got the whole world
In the palm of His hand
Who would sacrifice
Every drop of their blood
To pay the full price
Jesus did
Who would give love
When we don't deserve it
Only one, I'm sure of
Jesus would

Psalm 5:11

But let all who take refuge in you be glad; let them ever sing for joy. Spread your protection over them, that those who love your name may rejoice in you.

That Place Called Joy

Why do you worry
Want answers in a hurry
Be patient, Jesus will help you
Doubt will cause resistance
Speak it into existence
Keep praying, till answers come through
Your faith seems lacking
When the devil's attacking
Ask Jesus to come strengthen you
Keep on believing
To be receiving
Faith is the substance to cling to
Sometimes, you've got to walk a valley
Climb hard up a steep mountain
Before you reach that place called joy
So, keep on moving forward
Fighting, heading toward it
You'll make it to that place called joy
I will be praying
Your name, I'll be saying
Lifting you higher to God's throne
Praying is where to start
To heal a worried heart
And have joy, like never known

1 Samuel 2:9

He will guard the feet of his faithful servants, but the wicked will be silenced in the place of darkness. "It is not by strength that one prevails;

The Servant

I am just a servant
My Master is the Lord
He saved my life, I'm grateful
Serving Him is such a small meager reward

I wake up each morning
Seeking first, My Master's Word
His instructions prepare me
Tribulations are coming, I've heard

Knowing who I was
I feel so ill equipped
For my mind is weak in thought
I'm unworthy to serve Him, I'll admit

But He loves me anyway
He forgave me of my sins
I am humbled before my Master
And I will serve Him without end

Mark 10:52

"Go," said Jesus, "your faith has healed you." Immediately he received his sight and followed Jesus along the road.

I Follow His Light

My shadow reminds me
Of my dark past
It follows me around
As I do my tasks
To live like the past
Wouldn't be right
Since I've known Jesus
I follow His Light
My shadow was blended
Right in with the dark
I didn't recognize
What had hold of my heart
One day I felt like
I was heading to hell
Desperate, I cried out
"Lord, save me," I yelled
My shadow knows me
Where I have been
It knows my dark secrets
And all of my sins
It knows my Savior
And stays behind me
As I walk toward His Light
That's in front of me
Jesus is now
Lord of my life
He changed my whole world
I follow His Light

Isaiah 41:10

So do not fear, for I am with you; do not be dismayed, for I am your God. I will strengthen you and help you; I will uphold you with my righteous right hand.

The Lord's Light

When you hear, the horror in the news
When you hear, how many die today
Each day, the future coming looks too dark
Ask Jesus Christ to come light up the way
When you hear, the rumors of another war
When you hear, the death toll in a fight
Don't run and hide, wear the armor of God
There's victory, in Jesus and His Light
Fear not the dark
That the world is covered by
Fear not the dark
That dwells in evil hearts
Fear not the dark
That tries to hide the truth with lies
Instead look for
The Lord's Light in the dark
When you hear, countries have been destroyed
When you hear, people have lost their homes
Pray for them, pray peace will come to all
The only peace to last is from God's throne
When you hear, people have no food to eat
When you hear, there's no hope left in sight
We can't give up, pray for the Lord to come
There's victory in Jesus and His Light

Psalm 62:5

Yes, my soul, find rest in God; my hope comes from him.

I Found Him

I took a road
That led the wrong way
Crashed into hell
Those were my darkest days
The bed, I made
I had to sleep in
Life was a nightmare
All because of sin
It took too much of
Drugs and booze
To find out those were
The wrong things to choose
But some mistakes
Help you win, instead of lose
When my life was looking grim
Is when I found Him
There are crossroads
Everywhere you go
Before you turn
Better turn to God, to know
With temptations
The devil sets his snares
Choose wise, my friends
Start each day with prayer

Lamentations 3:25

The Lord is good to those whose hope is in him, to the one who seeks him;

I've Been Needing You

I've been needing You
For a long, long time
How could I've been so blind
I've tried living my way
Things didn't work well
I see now, I could only fail
I've been needing You
Jesus, my Lord
I've been needing You
As the main part of my life
To help me face all the strife
Lord, I'm stubborn
Stubborn, like a mule
I see now, I was a fool
I've been needing You
Jesus, my Lord
I've been needing You
Come dwell in my heart
Let Your light conquer my dark
I'm tired, so tired
Of losing, day after day
I see now, You are the Way
I've been needing You
Jesus, my Lord

Psalm 6:9

The Lord has heard my cry for mercy; the Lord accepts my prayer.

It's Time to Pray

All week, you've worried
Don't know what to do
You've tried everything you can
You need an answer
But you have no hope
Life didn't go as you planned
You never talk to God
You think He is a myth
Maybe you're believing a lie
The way your life's going
You're desperate now
You need to give God a try
It's time to pray
You should have done it long ago
It's time to pray
Don't question what you don't know
It's time to pray
Ask Jesus to show the way
Then when you wake up in the morning
It's time to pray
At night you think a lot
Regretting your past life
Wishing you had lived a different way
We've all have made mistakes
But forgiveness can be had
Just turn to Jesus and pray

Hebrews 9:15

For this reason Christ is the mediator of a new covenant, that those who are called may receive the promised eternal inheritance; now that he has died as a ransom to set them free from the sins committed under the first covenant.

For All My Mistakes

I ain't no good
Don't have what it takes
Why am I here
Am I a mistake

I am a fool
Fell for Satan's bait
Could have paid, dearly
For all my mistakes

I thank You, Jesus
For Your cleansing blood
You took this sinner
And cleaned off the mud
Bled cause of me
My sins were the stakes
You died on the cross
For all my mistakes

After I die
And see Heaven's gate
I'll be forever grateful
Make no mistake

1 Peter 1:24

For, "All people are like grass, and all their glory is like the flowers of the field; the grass withers and the flowers fall,

We're Just Passing Through

Come tomorrow
We might not be living here
We weren't promised
But tomorrow, we shouldn't fear
Life doesn't last
We should seek higher ground
Cause this ain't home, it's true
We're just passing through

Come one's death
When they're no longer here
Grieve for them
But only a few tears
Remember good times
And their smiling face
But this ain't home, it's true
We're just passing through

Life is short
Shorter, than you think
You'll grow old
And that's what really stinks
So dance, long as you can
One day, the song will end for you
C'est la vie
We're just passing through

Come, what may
Sometimes life's really hard
You'll get a lousy hand
Still, you have to play your cards
Some live for decades
Some will live, a day or two
But we'll all go home, it's true
Cause we're just passing through

Jeremiah 15:11

The Lord said, "Surely I will deliver you for a good purpose; surely I will make your enemies plead with you in times of disaster and times of distress.

You're Special in God's Eyes

You're beautiful
When you smile, I smile too
I love your presence
And talking to you
You are sunshine
With a loving heart
You light up strangers
Whose lives are dark

You have a purpose
I believe you're gifted
You have a talent
Touching lives that need lifted
But there are days
You'll withdraw out of sight
God needs you
The world needs your light

Sometimes you're sad
When life is going wrong
You've made mistakes
You don't think you belong
That's just the devil
Don't you listen to his lies
His attacks come, as no surprise
You're special in God's eyes

We all need help
Somedays we're not so strong
We can't give up
Our sadness won't last long
I'll lift you up
When your spirit's flying low
You'll do the same
When I'm sad, I know

Proverbs 19:21

Many are the plans in a person's heart, but it is the Lord's purpose that prevails.

As It's Meant To Be

In the beginning
When God made this world
Paradise was perfect
As each day unfurled
Then came the devil
Temptation, his game
Man fell right for it
Now, nothing's the same
Mankind has suffered
With diseases and war
Everything's perverted
Worse more than before
True joy is drifting
Feels distant each day
Tears keep increasing
The hopeful, still pray
But healing is coming
Across every land
When Jesus appears
As per God's plan
Believers will rise up
Slaves will be free
Paradise will return
As it's meant to be

2 Corinthians 9:12

This service that you perform is not only supplying the needs of the Lord's people but is also overflowing in many expressions of thanks to God.

What Are You Waiting For

Do you know someone
Who is hurting deep inside
Do you watch them
Knowing, there's pain they hide
They need a light
To shine in their dark
They need you and God
To shine in their heart
Go on
What are you waiting for

Don't let another day
Come and go by
Tonight may be too late
As they'll go home to cry
They need a light
To break through their dark
They need you and God
To shine in their heart
Go on
What are you waiting for

Make a difference
In someone else's life
Give them hope
In the storm of their strife
We all need help
When everything looks grim
Even you were once like them
Go on
What are you waiting for

If someone's problem
Is heavy on your mind
Maybe that's God
Saying, "Help them, it's time."
Become a light
To shine in their dark
They need you and God
To shine in their heart
Go on
What are you waiting for

Psalm 109:26

Help me, Lord my God; save me according to your unfailing love.

Hey, Jesus

Another night
Of drinking in a bar
Drunk, once again
Too drunk to drive my car
I'll feel ashamed
When I wake up around noon
Its closing time
And I say to the moon
I'm a sinner
Who struggles in every way
Will I see angels
In Heaven, one fine day
They say, find Jesus
He is the only way
Hey, Jesus
Where are you
This alcoholic
Sure does need You
Another night
I have let myself down
Drinking, too much
But not enough to drown
I want to quit
Again, I've gone too far
Damn alcohol
And I say to the stars
I'm a sinner

Who struggles in every way
Will I see angels
In Heaven, one fine day
They say, find Jesus
He is the only way
Hey, Jesus
Where are you
This alcoholic
Sure does need You
Another night
I lay in my bed
Drunk, once again
Wishing, I was dead
My pillow knows
Every tear, I've cried
Tonight it hears
Help Jesus, I tried

John 1:29

The next day John saw Jesus coming toward him and said, "Look, the Lamb of God, who takes away the sin of the world!

Jesus Gives His All

Just one drop
Is all it would take
To save us all
From our own damned fate
But Jesus bled
Till He had no more blood
Out of love
He gave His all
Yes, Jesus gives His all

Just one chance
Is all He'd like to give
To save us all
To go to Heaven and live
But we're fools
We need every chance there is
Out of love
He gives them all
Yes, Jesus gives them all

Smart is the fool
When his back's against the wall
That prays to Jesus
To send in a wrecking ball
To tear it down

So, the fool can start again
Jesus loves
And fools can win
Yes, fools like me can win

Just one time
Jesus came here to die
To save us all
From the devil and his lies
If you'll believe
Let Jesus in your heart
Then, you'll see
He gives His all
Yes, Jesus gives His all

Psalm 44:3

It was not by their sword that they won the land, nor did their arm bring them victory; it was your right hand, your arm, and the light of your face, for you loved them.

I Am Loved

I'm greatly blessed
Much more than I deserve
I have troubles
No more than I can take
I have grace
To live on, everyday
I am loved
In a mighty way
I have mercy
New, with the morning dew
I have a future
Where my dreams come true
I am grateful
I want to praise Him, all day
I am loved
In a mighty way
I don't know what I would do
If Jesus wasn't in my heart
I've live without Him before
At a time, when my life was dark
I have His Light
To see in the dark
I have a hope
Expecting greater things
My soul is His
I am saved, I can say
I am loved
In a mighty way

John 1

In the beginning was the Word, and the Word was with God, and the Word was God. He was with God in the Beginning. Through him all things were made; without him nothing was made that has been made.

Each Page is You

I can't fail the lessons
Or be second guessing
Not You, my Lord
The Bible tells me what to do
The scriptures still are true
They are, my Lord

All I need to succeed
Is read and be like You
Your Word can't age
There's truth on every page
Cause each page is You

You were the Word made flesh
You spoke and we were blessed
Thank You, my Lord
If Your Word was not true
By now, there'd be something new
There's not, my Lord

All we need to succeed
Is read and be like You
Your Word can't age
There's truth on every page
Cause each page is You

Matthew 14:31

Immediately Jesus reached out his hand and caught him. "You of little faith, " he said, "why did you doubt?"

Build My Faith

Hear me, God
Oh, how I need you
I'm lost these days
To know what to do
My faith's weak
Help me find my way
Stay close to me
Strengthen me, I pray

Build my faith
To move mountains
Build my faith
To beat all odds
Build my faith
To face, bad storms
Build my faith
In You, my God

Can't go back
To how I used to be
I know there's a life
Better for me
Hear my prayer
You know what I lack
God, more than ever
I need my faith back

Deuteronomy 31:6

Be strong and courageous. Do not be afraid or terrified because of them, for the Lord your God goes with you; he will never leave you nor forsake you.

Courage

There is courage in His Word
There is courage in His Name
There is courage found in prayer
There is courage to be claimed
There is courage in your faith
There is courage when there's fear
Receive your courage from Jesus
Believe, He is always near

2 Chronicles 6:4

Then he said: "Praise be to the Lord, the God of Israel, who with his hands has fulfilled what he promised with his mouth to my father David.

God's Hands

I am grateful for God's hands
To help me up when I fall down
I am grateful for God's hands
To hold me up and stand my ground
I will not fear
No, I won't fear
I know His hands
Are always near
Protecting me and healing me
I am thankful for God's hands

Psalm 17:7

Show me the wonders of your great love, you who save by your right hand those who take refuge in you from their foes.

Love Can Save the Day

People are crying
Many hearts are sad
They have no hope
Tomorrow looks bad
The world is moaning
Everywhere there's war
Will hate ever end
We can't take much more
If we believe
If we all would pray
Maybe there is a chance
Love can save the day
We can't keep fighting
Keep living this way
Let's love each other
Love can save the day
Brother against brother
Blood keeps on spilling
Stop playing the cards
The devil's dealing
There are no winners
Everyone will lose
Unless we preach, love
Is the only choice to choose

1 Thessalonians 4:17

After that, we who are still alive and are left will be caught up together with them in the clouds to meet the Lord in the air. And so we will be with the Lord forever.

A Day is Coming

A day is coming
A day of celebration
Jesus is coming
To take us home

A day is coming
A day for rejoicing
Jesus is coming
To take us home

Better get ready
Today, could be the day
Better get ready
Jesus is on His way
No one knows, but God
Which day, will be the day
All I know is, I'm ready
To go home, I can't stay

A day is coming
A day, God promised
Jesus is coming
To take us home

Psalm 63:3

Because your love is better than life, my lips will glorify you.

To a Better Place

Are you weary
Are you depressed
Could you just cry and cry
Cause everything's a mess
Don't you give up
I know someone you need
His name is Jesus Christ
He's your only hope from here
To a better place
I was like you
I had no hope
I struggled, day after day
Numbed my pain to cope
Then, I met Him
And my life was changed
Jesus saved me from hell
Gave my feet a path to travel
To a better place
Now, bow your head
We're going to pray
Receive Jesus in your heart
For a new life, today
Start looking up
Your hope is in His Name
Ask Him to lead the way
He'll open doors for you
To a better place

Revelation 3:20

Here I am! I stand at the door and knock. If anyone hears my voice and opens the door, I will come in and eat with that person, and they with me.

Open the Door

Jesus is knocking, again
At your door, my friend
Give Him at least one chance
Open the door
You're hesitating, again
You won't let Jesus in
Why, when your heart says
Open the door
Let go of your old pride
Look on the other side
You'll see a different light
Open the door
You have done things, you hate
Shame is a heavy weight
Jesus can lighten your load
Open the door
Jesus can make you whole
He wants to save your soul
Don't give, a second thought
Open up the door
You won't have no regret
It is time, you two met
Wait no more, turn the lock
Open the door

Jeremiah 29:11

For I know the plans I have for you, "declares the Lord, "plans to prosper you and not to harm you, plans to give you hope and a future.

His Plan

I can't wait
Until each new day
I'm very hopeful
What I will see
God has a plan
It is a good one
He has created
To give to me
Beyond my sight
And expectations
Past the horizon
There is God's plan
If I believe
Live by my faith
Trust God, completely
I'll live His plan
Every morning
I have to thank God
He has been good
Always, to me
He has saved me
For something special
I get excited
Wondering, what it'll be

Psalm 86:13

For great is your love toward me; you have delivered me from the depths, from the realm of the dead.

The Depth of Your Love

Lord, they don't know You
Forgive them, Savior
Open their blind eyes
To see who You are
I was like them
But now my heart knows You
Help me explain
The depth of Your love
Lord, they don't know You
And Your compassion
You have new mercy
To shine on their souls
Greater are You
Than what they are facing
Reveal Your heart
The depth of Your love
Lord, they don't know You
That is our mission
To lead all others
To You, Jesus Christ
Let Your Kingdom come
To each hopeful heart
So, they will feel
The depth of Your love

Matthew 21:22

If you believe, you will receive whatever you ask for in prayer."

We're Going to Pray

I can see there's pain
Deep in your eyes
It's time to face the truth
Live no more lies
Your heart's breaking
Why don't you admit it
This life you're living
Why don't you quit it

We're going to pray
I know a better way
I use to be like you
Addiction ain't nothing new
You're trapped in deceit
Don't you feel any defeat
This life, you can't win
But you can start again
Jesus is the only way
We're going to pray

How many more times
Will you try and fail
How many more days
Will you spend in jail
You're gambling your life
You're going to lose
But you don't have to
There's a new road to choose

We're going to pray
I know a better way
I use to be like you
Addiction ain't nothing new
You're trapped in deceit
Don't you feel any defeat
This life, you can't win
But you can start again
Jesus is the only way
We're going to pray

Exodus 23:20

See, I am sending an angel ahead of you to guard you along the way and to bring you to the place I have prepared.

Angels, Among Us

God has angels that He sends us
Who will come fast to our aid
They'll move closer, right beside us
Every time, scripture is prayed
Where we gather, pray in His Name
In our midst, Jesus is there
There're also angels, who will join in
To agree with us in prayer

Let us thank God for His angels
All the angels, among us
They protect us, while we live here
Till the day we see Jesus

There's an army, hedge of protection
If we have faith and boldly pray
Never give up, keep on fighting
There're more angels on their way
A day is coming, with rejoicing
We won't have to fight no more
Down on earth and high in Heaven
Angels will sing, forevermore

1 Thessalonians 3:10

Night and day we pray most earnestly that we may see you again and supply what is lacking in your faith.

Pray Without Ceasing

Never stop praying
Don't give up, keep praying
God's help is on the way
Your words have power
To bring forth, God's power
Always pray, each day

Amen is the word, we say at the end
It's the turning point, where answers begin
So, keep faith increasing
And pray without ceasing
God's Word says, we're going to win

I'm praying for you
If you'll pray for me, too
Together, we can be strong
Soon, in one accord
We'll sing to our Lord
With joy, our victory song

Amen is the word, we say at the end
It's the turning point, where answers begin
So, keep faith increasing
And pray without ceasing

Job 33:14

For God does speak- now one way, now another- though no one perceives it.

Talk to Me God

Talk to me God
I need to hear from You
Talk to me God
I don't know what to do
I'm scared
I feel alone
This loneliness
I've never known
I know
You are out there
I need You here
Answer my prayer
Talk to me God
I need to hear from You

Psalm 67:6

The land yields its harvest; God, our God blesses us.

God Blesses Me

God blesses me more than I give thanks
He blesses me more than I can count
Blessing after blessing
Favor after favor
God loves me so much
He gave me a Savior
My heart is overflowing
My soul is ever glowing
Because my God blesses me
Thank You, God

Psalm 42:1

As the deer pants for streams of water, so my soul pants for you, my God.

From The Cross

Raindrops are on my windows
The windows of my soul
As the rain falls from the pain
I wish my life could be whole

I have most of my broken pieces
But lost some along the way
I can't change a thing from the past
But I can be reborn, they say

So, here I am, Jesus
Take what's left of me
Repurpose me, as You please
Life brought me to my knees
Lift me up from the ashes
Restore the good things, I've lost
Lead me to higher ground
As I start over from the cross

I've seen others change their lives
I believe, there's hope for me
Once, I get rid of these old chains
I can love me again and live free

1 Corinthians 1:27

But God chose the foolish things of the world to shame the wise; God chose the weak things of the world to shame the strong.

No One Else

I was too blind to see
How much He had loved me
I didn't believe, He heard my prayers
The old devil had me bluffed
I didn't feel good enough
But I was wrong, He had always cared

Now, that I know, I can't let go
He saved me from myself
What comes at me, I have victory
With Jesus and no one else
I didn't hear what was preached
He's always been in reach
I have regretted every wasted day

I can't make up lost time
But I'll shout at the finish line
Jesus is life, the truth and way
Now, that I know and I can't let go
He saved me from myself
What comes at me, I have victory
With Jesus and no one else

Proverbs 14:23

All hard work brings a profit, but mere talk leads only to poverty.

There Will Always Be Another Mountain

There will always be another mountain
After climbing the one you're on
There will always be another struggle
Until you reach, your final home
To be surefooted, keep looking up
Toward the Son, shining over the peak
Seek Jesus for hope with each step
He is your strength, when you are weak
There will always be another mountain
Some are higher than the ones before
There will always be disappointments
That break your heart and make you sore
But stand up and brush yourself off
Ask for mercy and start climbing again
God is with you, through every trial
Trust in Him every day to the end
There will always be another mountain
Keep rejoicing as you work and sweat
Hard work will bring you rewards
Instead of sorrow and regrets
When you reach the mountain's summit
Praise God and tell Him, Thank You
Take a moment to catch your breath
Look around and enjoy the view

Exodus 20:3

You shall have no other gods before me.

I Changed My God

You should've of seen me years ago
I was someone you wouldn't know
I was an addict, a sorry mess
I hated my life, I must confess
I use to think of no one else
Only serving, my selfish self
I didn't care what others thought
Seeking pleasure, is what I sought
Why I'm still here, amazes me
It's not by chance, I beat the odds
I should've died long time ago
The only reason, I changed my God

Matthew 8:11

I say to you that many will come from the east and the west, and will take their places at the feast with Abraham, Isaac, and Jacob in the kingdom of heaven.

Come Take Us Home

God gave us tears
So we could cry, as needed
When we are sad
Or great joy comes to us
God rather see
Our tears to be from gladness
One day, they will
When Jesus comes for us
Cause tears of joy
To everyone, our Lord
Come take us home
Come take us home
We are so sad
From what the world's become
Come take us home
Come take us home
Oh, what a day
When we will see our Savior
Shine through the clouds
As all His angels sing
We will rejoice
As our spirits are lifted
Up to the clouds
To go home with our King

2 Chronicles 33:13

And when he prayed to him, the Lord was moved by his entreaty and listened to his plea; so he brought him back to Jerusalem and to his kingdom. Then Manasseh knew that the Lord is God.

He Is Moved

God's love for me
Is like the ocean waters
I see, so far
But there's much more out there
I stand in awe
Upon the shore and wonder
Why He loves me
Why does He even care

Then, from nowhere
A seagull lands by me
And I am moved
My heart is moved
He follows me
Hoping I'll bless him
And I am moved
My heart is moved

Much like the bird
If I draw close to God
He'll notice me
And see, I seek His love
Then, He'll be moved
He will greatly bless me
Cause God loves me
More than, I know of

So, I give praise
To God for His love
And He is moved
God's heart is moved
I'll follow Him
Knowing He loves me
And He is moved
God's heart is moved

John 11:35

Jesus wept.

Jesus Wept

The moment when Jesus was born
Before He nursed and slept
He knew right then, why God sent Him
The baby Jesus wept

He lived His youth in Nazareth
Was wiser, than His years
He felt the grief that people had
He wept, when they had tears

Jesus came to build a church
His mission here was clear
He became the cornerstone
The mortar, blood and tears

Jesus wept, cause of our sin
Tears came from pain and love
He cried, then died, upon the cross
Lost souls, He kept thought of

Immanuel was here on earth
God's promises are kept
Our Savior came to save the world
For mankind, Jesus wept

Romans 8:25

But if we hope for what we do not yet have, we wait for it patiently.

It's Only Going to Get Better

It's going to get better
Just wait and see
No matter, the weather
Cause God loves me
I'm all prayed up
For any storm
I'm not worried
Whatever forms
If it rained forty days
And forty nights
All my faith is in God
To make things right
It's only going to get better
Made up my mind
I believe, with all my heart
The sun will shine

Psalm 27:14

Wait for the Lord; be strong and take heart and wait for the Lord.

Pray and Wait

You're exhausted
You can't go on
All you've tried
Has gone wrong
Your burdens weigh
Much on your back
The strength you need
You always lack
Give it to God
He'll help you through
When you don't know
What to do
If you're confused
Which path to take
Don't take a chance
Pray and wait
It's the darkest
Before first light
But if we wait
Till the time's right
The sun will rise
Colors increase
Well worth the wait
For God's masterpiece

Matthew 8:26

He replied, "you of little faith, why are you so afraid?" Then he got up and rebuked the winds and the waves, and it was completely calm.

Speak To the Mountain

Lord, come dry my tears
Lord, calm all my fears
Speak to the ocean
Make it smooth
Speak to the mountain
Make it move
Lord, I'm so afraid
Lord, come to my aid
Speak to the ocean
Make it smooth
Speak to the mountain
Make it move

You're my strength, to be strong
You're my hope, to go on
You're my light, so I can see
Thank You, Lord, for loving me
You're my joy, when I'm sad
You're my grace, when I'm mad
You're my Master, yet I'm free
Thank You, Lord, for loving me

Psalm 37:23

The Lord makes firm the steps of the one who delights in him.

A Little Step

A leap of faith
Most times can be
A little step
Though, you can't see
Hindsight is clearer
Once, you're there
The struggles over
An answered prayer

If a large mountain
Stands in your way
Look at the summit
Have faith and pray
Then, take a step
Toward the peak
A little step toward God
Is a mighty leap

Psalm 136:3

Give thanks to the Lord of lords: his love endures forever.

There's Not a Better Choice Out There

This old world has temptations
I've tried many in the past
They've all lead me nowhere
They're a waste, they never last
People said, try this or that
They're just fools, who don't care
Don't become, like I once was
Don't get caught by their snares
Of all the things, I've ever tried
Jesus is the one, I'll share
He has everything to offer
There's not a better choice out there
So, if you're living with a bad choice
Thinking, that life is unfair
Let me turn you on to Jesus
There's not a better choice out there
There's a lot of smoke and mirrors
To confuse you, everyday
If you want to know the real truth
Follow Jesus, live His way
I'm not trying to mislead you
Toward a dead end or the dark
I want to show His Light to you
That is shining in my heart

1 Peter 1:23

For you have been born again, not of perishable seed, but of imperishable, through the living and enduring word of God.

Better Than New

If you knew me, years ago
I was a broken, pile of mess
Wasted, living in the gutter
A man seeing hopelessness

I was low, as one can get
Many nights I cried and drank
I wondered why I should live on
I hit bottom, my spirit sank

In desperation and despair
I cried out, "Jesus, please save me"
He reached down into my darkness
Gave me hope and made me free

I was, once, a dead man walking
God knows, the hell I went through
Now, I'm healed, because of Jesus
He made me, better than new

John 10:10

The thief comes only to steal and kill and destroy; I have come that they may have life, and have it to the full.

Enjoy Your Life

I had a friend, who would tell me
This simple phrase, "Enjoy your life"
His words pierced my calloused heart
Hardened by hardships and strife
Knowing this man, from our talks
And the struggles, he'd gone through
I asked, "How do you enjoy your life?
Tell me, so I will know, too."
He said, "First, you must seek God
And follow Jesus, every day.
Count your blessings and give thanks.
Be humble, have faith, and pray.
Surrender everything to God.
If you'll do this, with your wife,
You'll see things a different way.
Then you can enjoy your life.
I was there, when my friend died
He left with a smile on his face
There was no doubt, where he went
He's living in a better place
From time to time, I think of Him
Still, his laughter can be heard
Well, old friend, "Enjoy your life"
Thanks for your uplifting words

Luke 6:31

Do to others as you would have them do to you.

Have You Ever Been Stoned

People judged me in the past
When I was a lost soul
They'd throw insults like stones
Their words made in me holes
I bled from all my wounds
But I survived my fall
When Jesus came and saved me
Saved me from it all
Have you ever been stoned
Has someone hit you with their words
Forgive them and move on
There are wiser words to be heard
Before you throw stones at someone
Best throw some at yourself
Let God be the judge of them
Instead by someone else
Led the lost to the Savior
When you see someone fall
Let Jesus come and save them
Save them from it all
Have you ever been stoned
Has someone hit you with their words
Forgive them and move on
There are wiser words to be heard

John 14:6

Jesus answered, "I am the way and the truth and the life. No one comes to the Father except through me.

Make Today Be the Day

Why still live the way you are
The road you're on is a dead end
You can walk it to nowhere
Your soul knows you'll never win
You hurt the ones, who love you most
You live unsure about yourself
Deep inside you want to change
You're scared of being someone else
Life would be a whole lot better
If you'd talk to God and pray
He'll help you get rid of demons
Make today be the day
You weren't made to live in darkness
Step into the light and say
Jesus, be Lord of my life
Make today be the day
I've walked down the road you're on
I thank God, I turned around
Now, I walk the road with Jesus
I smile more, than I frown
So you'll know, I pray for you
I love you and my heart cares
Until you live to follow Jesus
You'll always be in my prayers

Psalm 62:12

And with you, Lord, is unfailing love; and, you reward everyone according to what they have done.

Empty Pockets

I was born with nothing into a world of strife
I was given some pockets to carry through life
They said, fill your pockets to show your success
I did like they told me to succeed their test
Many great things, I gathered and kept
My pockets grew bigger, increasing in depth
Little did I know, how heavy things are
Possessions become burdens that take one, so far
I received less joy from things I possessed
I searched for answers, why I was sad with success
A wise man said, my spirit would never be content
If I didn't know Jesus and the Holy Spirit, God sent
So, I sought after Jesus, I had nothing to lose
I learned how to live, after hearing His News
I started empting my pockets of things I had
As my pockets became lighter, the less I felt sad
I discovered the more I gave, the happier I became
So, I gave my life to Jesus, now, I'm not the same
When I leave this world to go live with the Lord
I'll leave empty pockets for a much greater reward